LIGHT'S ASCENT

Stories and Poems

Andrew Moo

Miami, FL

Light's Ascent: Stories and Poems

Address inquiries to the publisher:

Atom Publications
Miami, Florida

ISBN for print: 978-1-63452-722-4
ISBN for e-book: 978-163452-723-1

Library of Congress Control Number: 2015902518

Printed in the United States of America

Cover by Melissa Phillips for Allwrite Communications, Inc.

DEDICATION

To my wife and other friends

CONTENTS

I

STORIES

1

If you know love,
You speak all languages.

2

Excellency, I know what you are
But what do you do?

3

New ways and things unseen,
God would not intervene.

4

The thin line between love and hate:
The space between nine and eight.

5

Shakespeare, Francis of Assisi, Dickinson:
One was good, one was wise, one was fun:
Which one was which one was which one?

6

Humble, practical, sublime, loving:
If you are nice, you can do anything.

7

Estoy aquí, no "soy aquí."
¿Quién eres tú?.

8

Success or disaster,
Marriage is an act of God.

9

Maturity:
"Knowing right from wrong
And choosing the right."

10

Divorce:
"So easy to fall in love,
Ever so hard to love."

11

At your feet, humility
In your face, beauty.

12

María & José passed the test
But Jesús didn't.

13

Give now or give later.
Receive graciously, then share.

14

Computers are only human:
Sometimes I think they are out of their minds.

15

Ce matin de gentillesse
Ce soir, c'est perfection.

16

Love moderately:
Amo, amas, amat.
Learn a language with love.

17

La pregunta:
¿Ser o estar?
Esa es la cuestión.

18

Adam: "That apple gave me gas."
Eve: "Darn it! We don't have Pepto-Bismol."

19

It's freezing!
This must be Paradise.

20

The Arts of Law & Medicine:
Please Apply Within.

21

"If you miss her now,
by the time you leave,
you will have missed her
completely."

22

School:
If you pass, you're good.
If you fail, it's the teacher.

23

Let me decide:
In-laws or outlaws?
Let's embrace all laws.

24

Truth or silence:
The dilemma of those who are just.

25

Higher education:
The professors have a third eye
And the students, common sense.

26

She was charged with beauty:
Pre-trial, pre-duckling, pre-swan.

27

One is greater than three or seven
Clearly Truth's ones abides in heaven.

28

I thoroughly love myself.
Now let me love my neighbor.

29

Disaster strikes.
Americans: Who's to blame? God.
The Japanese: Let's fix things. Good.
Jamaicans: You see it. God bless.

30

[With a Southern accent]
If I done you wrong,
I must do you right.

31

The soul has no religion:
The soul belongs to God.

32

She said, "Go to hell"
And I did. It was all right
Except for the sunburn.

33

Orthography:
The art of knowing
Who is who
And what is what.

34

Hell is a forced vacation:
The idle rich, the idle poor.
Happy is the man in between.

35

"Please" takes you to the king. "Of course."
"Thank you" is the key to paradise. "You're welcome."

36

The innocent prisoner escaped
But the prison wouldn't let him back in.

37

"You are rich!"
"No, my father is."

38

"Sais-tu que tu es éternel?"
"Je ne le crois pas."
"Tu verras."

39

Laundry:
When you've got things,
"You have to keep them clean."

40

Zero talents: delusion.
Dirt poor: allusion.

41

Feet on the ground:
Hell or paradise?

42

In middle and high school
Once cool but twice the fool.

43

American time: Ten minutes before.
Jamaican time: Just around the corner.
Latin time: Again, who are you?.

44

Rastafarians:
They believed in him
But didn't believe him.

45

Misericordia y miseria:
¿Cuál es la diferencia? No sé
Tal vez, el corazón.

46

That man traveled far
To find himself.

47

Justice is the blind carbon copy
Of love, happiness, and co-existence.

48

Every religion, large or small,
Has a moral system.
Am I right or wrong?

49

A shaman and a witch too:
I dedicate my life to you.

50

If you are a student, you do well.
If you are a saint, you do good.

51

The first sign of a doctor:
Cure a cold.

52

I love but don't feel worthy:
I fall short, so I won't be wordy.

53

Gita, Bible, Qur'án:
Yes, they are truly One.

54

Only love can save you
On your wedding day.

55

Instant karma:
It's a matter of hearts and numbers.

56

This man went home
To study film.

57

When was the Civil War
A civil war?
In *Virginia City*.

58

Casablanca:
Ilsa loved them both.
Rick loved them all.

59

Culinary arts:
It's easier to prepare a feast
Than a dinner for one.

60

Enseigner:
Regardez les yeux,
Écoutez le coeur.

II

POEMS

HONG KONG

1964-1966

Ages 12-14

SING SADLY

A bird in the high and soundless
What voice on earth does it hear?

I

What a fickle wind tonight
In heaven as in heart:
It's music to weep by

My friend, I concede this dream:
Your sister is a gift of beauty
Destined for some other's eyes

Too clearly
My young silence will outlive
Her knowing and fade, untold
May I keep what's not been had?
Why hope in need of tears?

II

I write romance:
A common dream scales the forbidding walls
Of age and seeks the fair princess

He writes poor French
And his broken words have no meaning.
His note is thrown away.

In the streets, he sees her from afar
Quiet vision grows to quieter love
And love into intrigue

Behold, I bring a mystery to the sea
It grows with uneasy meaning
And bursts sudden in my eyes

III

Her name, launched upon the wind
Leaf-like descends
And steams the waters

Her smile flits
On the gleaming foam
And checks the wave so slightly

Her eyes dip and rise
Very clear, so eloquent
Yet speak with strange ambivalence

A pretty dream:
I could have seen the sun tonight.
He is but a friend.

She sees my thinking
But will translate no feeling,
Will stir no untimely fire

To put away the glow
I would marry two words: love, sacrifice
To unite what were born together

I must not turn from life
And the body will not exist alone
Now I have tasted beauty

Somehow, to give and give,
Happy in the night,
For each day pours freely of itself

IV

Tomorrow will arrive, silent,
I yearn to meditate in the first light
And burn with energy, love

And then, in the full sun's poetry

To live on when the whittled bits of self
Fall, careless, into fire

Live on, like the sea
Which courts the land
Oblivious of the weather
Not survive, no; surpass.
To laugh at me, and know better
The land, the sea

1975

KINGSTON, JAMAICA

1966-1971

Ages 14-20

AURORA AUSTRALIS (Australian Dawn)

Lost, I see her lost
Fidgeting with life, unknowing
Touched grime, and ran
Into escapist blue
Blue, unfeeling blue

And she wasn't fine
Within her move of gentleness
Spinning, she groped
But to give, but to give
Of deep responsive her. . .

Then his eyes,
They made light of rhythm,
Enriched, expanded her core
Made her inspire, shine

She, rising in this restful meaning
Dwelling in his life
Seeing depth, feeling warm
Feeling green in his teaching touch

Night words, they weep
Then laugh, for timeless length
And sleep, dream. . .
With morning colored, new
So it seems, refound

Kittens soft
Flower, red, smiles
And the sweat of sun
Ain't no burden

And moving easy
On a sidewalk, and not afraid
And there's morning
In her smile
And evening in her walk

Then to hear her speak
The sooth of feeling words
None too far, a touch away
In the aura of her slight shift
Of body
And deeper soul

1969

POINT 2 SATISFACTION

Eyes in eyes, I be blue
I see the twinkling in her eyes
That could, did hold my depth
In a craze

Is it her walk?
I see love all sent to me,
Hear words binding me
In some sweet precise feeling
As I cry in what I hurt. . .
I don't know

Floral nights, she goes away;
All tied to her, to positive move her
To innocence, with a certain power
In hoping
At twin thoughts embracing:
Blind togetherness

A small touch on the hand
Is with birth-revelations
The eyes see
But the intrinsic closes out

But hurt is less than the coming
Of a fruitless life,

Soul saying: Soul, I don't know
Don't wish to know, I want to live

A woman of greenest life will live by
No other kind of hovering warmth
At this, the hour of dawn:
Later I may cry if I love.

1969

SHATTERING THE LOVELESS BLUE

Of little love
that bloomed into whorls
of velvet sensation
when the need for varied warmth
bubbled into an empty mind,
of gentleness
and touching united
in sprouting feelings of the unknown.
Weak and receptive
is the burning, deeply whirling inside
to the fingertip
in waves that vary in adjustment
to the contact
of the hand, the perfume.

Come, syllables from within
(too many
for the mind knew no meaning)
circling, rushing round
the sweet disturbance that sings
stings the eyes to closing.
A change, life turns
certifies this soft living,
the inward crescendo swarming
to warm breathing, slow intake
drifting, pausing
in a world of certain silence:
Quietude that explodes.

1970

BOSTON, MASSACHUSETTS
USA

1972-1973

DEAR PATIENCE

It is past midnight
Yet she moves with the universe
Within the kind faces of her life
Her mind is brushed with joy-dust.

She whispers with inner whisper:
There is so much warmth
In elusive uncertainty.

1972

NEAR YOU

Near you, I sit at pleasant's side
And when you go away
You swim lively in my memory
Yes, in your silent way
You watered the flower of my need.

So sensitive, it's in your smile
And your eyes, they mirror harmony
Here's calmness, here's flow. . .
Summer hours cast so easily
Spring a simple joy in me.

1972

SWEET ANALOGY

You are the apple in my eye
a large but pleasant speck

Your body has the evenness
of the finest thermostat
fairing your easy warmth

Your fragrance exudes
from India and her tea

All in all, yours is the closeness
I would most appreciate
over a vanilla malt
or on a crowded streetcar

1972

FALL MEASURE

Part I

In our path
A hundred joys in waiting
And we must harvest them
Or flee and feel no more

Even if we close our eyes
Pre-winter feelings will have their way
No, your star-like heart will give
Of loving energy that I may live.

Part II

What flow takes us to the sea?
Beauty asks, from room to room
And quiet she leads me
From the shadows
Into twilight warmth.

Part III

No subtle phase, then tears
Please leave all masks alone
Allow me to find you
Real, full-radiant
Without hint of night chasing night
Then blinded in the day

So when life carries us to dawn
Ask not of darkness what he saw;
Think not of sleepers in their sleep

Nor the cost of sorrow by the pound

You and I, together and alone
Owe much laughter to this world
We'll be compassion in weary hours
And dancers in the light.

Part IV

You bid me taste
From the well of memories
In your eyes, such pretty cups
To store sorry waters

There's a flame
That would make vapor of our tears
Would melt all crystal-fears
Know that the flame is love.

Part V

Every season in her time
The day her dress
The night her gown. . .

Life planted in the spring

Blooms full-flower in fall
And desires me gather her
Before the cold and fallen snow

Yet it is love who gathers us
And measures us by wait
For in heaven, it is a rule
That strong hearts be tested
Long hours at its gate

Part VI

You are poetry laughing
Beauty born of breath
Heart to take wind and snow
Mind to pluck roses from the blue

Dizzy feeling in the dark
But full force, a nerve
Dark voices call you
Tortured lives pursue
But sell your sword
And bow to Peace in kindness

Part VII

I glide gently
Through your mind
A guest without needs
For all I want
Has been given me

Hesitate not, my flower
In yielding your life to love
For in so giving
You shall drink of light
And dance no more with shadows.

Part VIII

Wave upon wave
Full spirit in a fire
We give much to do much
And no one knows

Fame flies the mind too far
Word multiplies so fast
We need till fields silently
And breathe pure and kindly

Part IX

A night of possibles
My words, your eyes, full vibration
Yet the power is still to come
In our sounding one soul
With one field under one Sun
A field of all that is being and will be

If the world knew more
If she knew her heart
She would have sensed this hour.

1972

MYSTERY

smile

to these eyes

that often seek you out

in the garden of your words.

If I could hear your heart and know

that which would hold back its vital rhythm

from a flow of sweetness, then in my searching,

I would not disturb the kindly spirit of your favor.

In the morning, the dew comes to settle on this rose;

droplets show lightly on the petals, which so bend,

till the sun later kisses these tears away.

If you smile, you will preserve

this drop of kindness

from evaporation.

1973

UNE ANNÉE: PROBLÈMES D'AMOUR

Tu es si belle,
enfant de philosophie

Si tu vis
dans un autre monde,
il faut m'envoyer
une carte postale.

1973

NEW DAY (LAUGHIN')

We sift songs tonight
Yet hold to hours
Of the approaching Day

What's cast is lost
Knowing heart
Our arms hold
In comfort of the pain
The eyes of love see no fear

A man but just a man
Sees the sun, embraces vision
Woman, by the stream
Will she will to taste all feeling
And swim the waters, to win to love?

1973

BOSTON, MASS.

1974-1976

MEDITATION ON FIRE

All to the last
that last extends to ever
O pure are the weavings
of beauty who may enter any door
and create of love, anew

Fire, lit within my heart
your warmth suffices little
till my hands are open
and God looks upon my way.

1974

BY NOON

When the sun
first peeks into my eyes
I feel
you are equal enough
to awaken you
my friend;
I shake you
with inadequate words
I move you
with untranslated fervor;
this is not just any day.

By noon
we'll be one in warmth,
free, yet in our hearts
as members of one dance.
For this Day
(we were told some time ago)
belongs to God.

1974

ONE MOST BEAUTIFUL

Your heart's a stormy world
When, on this day, you think east:
Heart on heart, life to liberty
A smile for anger in their eyes
Such is the mind without pretense
And tears do flow their way. . .

O beauty, take this path:
Spread wide your arms of light
Say: In the Name of God
This one heart cries apart
Desiring peace in the land of hearts
O Lord, save this world from itself.

A song in the tempest
To delay fears, till fears are no more

Beauty, rest gentle
This world's life moves in the heart of One.

1975

REST FAITHFUL

Like a child, to never shift
from searching
for some slight innocence
and so like a man, to see
your tears
and not know how
to gather them

Too many voices, perfect
in their one the other
following, no sympathy
and you, being a woman,
they want to see you
sing and dance
or laugh with me

Ah, to a simple love,
let's talk of symmetry:
two kindnesses,
that you will stain my shoulder
with you tears

and that I'll flourish
as you weep;
your love stirs hope
and love, and more

Long hours before today
in your room, alone
you cast words at shy ceiling
yet they never touched the pain
what else was there to do
but sigh
then sleep, exhausted

Here, in this inspired tenderness
take shelter, rest
your weary soul, safe
in your tears, know:
light follows dew

1975

MY HEART

You wake at 4:30
And you cry

You are *my heart*
And I fear your beauty:
"Know that you are
In the heart of your heart."

Your sincerity meets the test:
France cannot pierce
Your mind or soul

Your words are spirit-gentle, so
All France is at your door

Even when the laughter ceases,
We remain friends.

1975

JOIE ETERNELLE: ONE SPIRIT AND ONE LIFE

"Therefore, O ye friends of God, ye must in perfect purity attain spiritual unity and agreement to a degree that ye may express one spirit and one life."

– Bahá'í Writings

I

O God, the light I love
Is the spark You give
To a fading fire.

II

Who speak kindly will endure,
Will outlive the night
And touch affection
At first light.

III

Once you said these words
"First, love God, then if it be wise, love me."

I fail your "first" and may
Never love!

But, who have loved, still live;
Bright-clear the flash,
Their self-fire makes
Hot implosion.

By such fire, some men die
To live anew, or still living
Build a House, then
Die therein.

Futility? Their children's eyes
Twin stars shining, foretell
The soon rising
Of the Sun.

Martyrs inspire much finer air
Than we who live and sigh;
But to so love, and breathe
To so love and die!

We live, O yes we live to cradle
This tender infant-world,
To shield it from the cutting-edge
Of its own desires.

IV

Is love substantial, for us to see and hold?
As warm and manifest as the Sun is love
But much too high, to warm
To grasp.

For love is a maze of splendor;
With every step, at every turn,
We love ourselves
To inebriating joy!

Within us burns our need
To make whole our harmony,
To play legato in our souls
And give love fluency.

Father's eyes guide the child
From its longing pain, so pitiful,
To waiting arms, soft embrace
And a word too beautiful. . .

Show us, Father, how to love
You, how to dissipate the mirage
Of volatile affections.
Permit us love,

A love that sends its roots
Like messengers seeking
Assurance, delight, and sustenance
From the hidden sources
Of life-giving water,
A love that spreads so wide its shelter
That no being is left outside
Its shade and prosperity –
Your love, Father, and my joy.

V

Patience: one hour before we say, my love
"The will of God will last."
Will it be an hour's worth
Of tears (we have kerchiefs enough)
Or smiles shining through, from within?
You look full-bright among the roses;
You need not worry about our guests' whispering,
Light talk is only air.

Fair, these signs that crown our life today,
Beautiful, the garden's flowers
Whose perfumes subtly blend
Then drift, as one, into eternity

1976

A FRIEND WILL COME

This pain
that takes you apart
and unravels your mind
is good.
This emptiness
clearing your soul
and letting go of joy
gives birth to love.
These tears,
each the coalescence
of a hundred feelings,
are flowers grown
on your rich, rich soil.

A friend will come
to help turn your pain aright,
water this dry valley,
and gather roses from your field.
He will not be long.

1976

CANNOT

Soul to soul:
But you deny what you think
And what you feel

I need your eyes, my friend,
Penetrating my soul,
Questioning this hour

You need my heart
To answer cool questions,
Your fevered call

Love carries little wait
But blindness
Will demystify
The respect, the feeling

1976

KINGSTON & PORT ANTONIO JAMAICA

1976-1983

OUT A RIDDIM

De woman in de yard
gawn mad fi de second time,
an a well know the de feelin'
Ole man madness
a drag har cross
de macca in har head.

De zinc top
a float de sounds
as she drap fustration
pon har man.
Woman tired
wid a visit now an den,
marriage pon har brain;
trus her fawardness
to tell de whole yard
dat pickney a walk with dawg,
trus him frighten
'bout weddin coss
an wrappin fe him grave.

Mek me shut de window:
G'night, Miss Fuss-Fuss.

Yu know woman en 'merica
a mek noise.

Say wha. . . man
an woman equal?
An wha. . .dem
ha fe get dem share?
A wey wish wey,
is plat 'gainst us, man.
De queen o' de house
gwine tek one step
pass cleanin' an typin'
a sen one royal shark
to bite the livin'
daylights out a us.
An bwoy, riddim hard;
bitter, bitter
it no sweet.

1976

THE DARKNESS MOVES

I

The sun went out
and my eyes,
will they ever see light again?
In minutes, they became
new citizens of the dark, aware
of half-friendly shadows:
not all darkness
is unkind; but I fall
at every chair,
and break a crystal glass,
struggling with the eastern wall
that blocks out the morning
(was it the eastern wall?)
I now taste nothing
but dust and tears.

II

Once I slept
and I was free
to dream and pretend.

A hot fire, they said,
is white, hot enough
to melt the steel shaft
that might cleave the mind in two,
cause me to forget
the moments I stole
from myself,
then calling my belovéd
a thief.
A game of hide-and-seek
but she who seeks
just won't play fair.

III

What time is it?
Still no light,
no light, no light.
I yearn for some sharp thing
(a pain, perhaps)
to prod me, tell me that I live;
feeling nothing
nothing to cry for
no sun again:
it must be night.

IV

A hermit tries to sing
his own funeral song,
a slow, clumsy melody
that the cave walls
refuse, flooding
the hollowness
that only he can hear.

V

I love the seven colors
that make the white
I love the light:
I love the things I lack
and shun the blues
that turn to black.

Sing while you breathe,
learn this new song:

However deep the darkness, it isn't real,
It is but a rumor about the light.
When shadows part, the lights reveal
The hate you held is the love that lasts,
The hate you held is the love that lasts.

1977

LEAF OF LIFE

Clinging near
the crisp rose,
a dew drop
softens,
not in your eyes or mine
but in the green
of the leaf
of you-and-me.
Rose will only feed
on the green exchange
of life for life,
all in all,
no safety
in numbers but three,
He-and-you-and-me;
God it was that gave
His love to leaves
and sparked some life
in trees.

1978

BEAUTY ON THE FAR SIDE

A wisp of night
and eyes that fear to see
beneath the dark or light
through the haze of birth or privilege
to find something human bubbling there

A wisp of day
to eyes torn from sleep __
a moment's uncertainty __
then bright gold and life-green
purple pansy and yellow dandelion
A dream, this __ no __
black hand touching white face
red voice embracing brown soul

The heart is one
the heart has won
blood strife is gone
blood brothers __ One

Dedicated to my grandfather, who took flight to the next life on August 18, 1977

NINE MEETING NINE

1. Sing the way you love,
   Go blind and hate tomorrow.

2. Yes, in magic and prophecy
   Heart penetrates the show.

3. Seal the pain, fair false unity. . .
   But the flood exalts the plain.

4. If not from joy, then for experience
   And if not now, then yesterday.

5. Day won't find it, isolate the night
   Uninform the flame, confess the light.

6. City-light wanting sunshine
   So guiltily runs the street – away.

7. Born in the dark, growing darker:
   Born in the morning, May day mourning.

8. Would that a vow at that Spot
   Were not stealing.

9. Who can puzzle, who can clear
   The moment, the desire, the fear?

1979

MIAMI, FLORIDA

1983 onwards

THE CANDLE: Heart Opening

Both ends aflame
this one in midnight hell,
a discordant, revolutionary, smoking gun. . .
the other in specious paradise,
a sweet-singing, devious, kind-curved houri. . .

A white-hot candle,
with both ends aflame:
our ends meet in the middle ground
of "whatever lies between them,"
undeviating heart, flowering
and tasting Glory.

1984

DAZE OF MY LIFE

I sleep the sleep
of justice and mercy:
East-compass-West

I dance the dance
of shadow and light:
Left-loves-Right

I sing the song
of Ancient and New:
little-by-little, day-by-day

May God give learning
and beauty and life
and surety and love

and distance and nearness
to my eyes, my ears,
my heart, my soul,

that Love may hug me
and delicately charm me,

that I may swim
in steamy waters
and do a medicinal dance
in the rain

1996

NORTHERN LIGHTS (Learning)

Freshman heart feels half the hours
half the hurt, half the uncertainty
yet feels new energy,
the moon's laughter

Sophomore mind shines
like a star in the universe
with this dynamo,
this sun of love

Junior tears flow
in the face of the enemy – time –
we must love our enemy,
now and tomorrow

Senior exams excite
the heart, the mind, the tears
memory, truth, justice stir,
so every test ends in sweetness

2005

MILADY

Hurrying to the castle
Milady sings a lullaby
And the child understands
For she speaks the vernacular

Arriving at the castle
Milady dances a jig
(The melody echoing in the highlands)
And the mind dances too

Sleeping in the castle
Milady dreams
Consoles the silence
Delivers the difference
Of night and day
Hands the keys to her life
To the watchman
Who knows what is sane
And what is beautiful

2006

THE NEAR BEAUTIFUL

Destiny and history,
the north and south poles of life

and love,
the rhythm of waking hours

The circadian cycle
twirls in the illusion
that our hearts beat
and intent is 9/10ths
of what we do

Destiny and history,
the night and day of existence
You smile to a distant star
and your laugh echoes
to the edge of the universe

2006

LOOKING BETTER

If I should lie
and tell the worst,
my eyes will be
all pain and no love.

If I should tie
the long twisted
words and nuances,
leave this sacred heart alone.

If I should sigh
and lose my wealth,
I will not beg,
I will not lie,
I will not die.

2007

NIGHT

The moon sleeps in awful splendor
But I rub my tearless eyes:
These stoic eyes will rain
And this stoic heart will pain.

Before sleep, you love me
On waking, you hate me
This slight shift is benighted,
And cynical eyes become sighted.

2014

CIARA'S HEART

"It is Heaven that sustains the Earth"
These are the words of Francesco d'Assisi
But they echo in Ciara's heart.

*Francesco = St. Francis
*Ciara = St. Clare of Assisi

2014

ETHER

I touch the shadow of your former self
I see the slivers of your mind
Studying the world's imperfections
But still loving human beauty

I feel the shivers of your laughter
While you see with your own eyes
Your inner truth, canceling the lie
That you have no luminosity, no candor

O pure and luminous one!

2015

www.ingramcontent.com/pod-product-compliance
Ingram Content Group UK Ltd.
Pitfield, Milton Keynes, MK11 3LW, UK
UKHW040012200726
13854UKWH00001B/162

9 781634 527224